eat, pray, share

CWR

Personal booklet

Daily reading notes:
Selwyn Hughes

Group discussion questions:
Andy Peck

Contents

Introduction   4

How to use   6

Session 1: Communion as community   8

Session 1 readings   11

Session 2: Communion as commemoration   16

Session 2 readings   19

Session 3: Communion as covenant   24

Session 3 readings   27

Session 4: Communion as celebration   32

Session 4 readings   35

Session 5: Communion as commitment   40

Session 5 readings   43

A word of
intro

I am of the opinion that some of the most significant moments of our lives happen whilst we are sitting at a table. We spend a great deal of time sitting at or around tables: the family breakfast table or dinner table, school tables, work tables, lecture tables and so on.

There is a play called *The Dining Room* in which just a few actors play many different parts. They re-enact all the things that go on around the dining table in the home of an average family: the arguments, the announcements, the experiences and the emotions – including surprise, joy, disappointment, misunderstanding, laughter and countless others! The play ends with just the grandfather and the grandson sitting together at the table, reflecting on these things as the stage lights fade to black and the curtain comes down.

duction

For us, when the curtain of time comes down and the Church is gathered together in eternity, one of the very first things we will see will be a table set for the celebration of the marriage supper of the Lamb. What a day that will be! No more death, sorrow, crying or tears. The great handkerchief of love will be taken out and every tear will be dried.

Let's explore the most amazing table of all, a prelude to this great feast to come. I hope that it will change what for some may have become ritual and routine, to be revived and refreshed.

In the DVD sessions and group questions we will look at Communion as community, commemoration, covenant, celebration and commitment. In the five weeks of daily readings in this booklet we will fully explore the Jewish Passover. Let a greater understanding of these ancient traditions grow your appreciation of the Lord's Supper today.

Sincerely yours, in His name,

Mick Brooks

Mick Brooks
Consulting Editor

How to use

This resource is designed to include all you will need for five small group sessions. It comprises five DVD clips, group discussion questions based on each clip and Bible readings to be used between each session.

Preparation

1. Watch the week's DVD session before the meeting.

2. Select the questions you think would be most useful for your group to look at. You may want to use them all, depending on the time you have available. We suggest you plan for 30–45 minutes.

The session

1. Play the DVD clip first and go straight into the icebreaker question.

2. Discuss the questions you have selected.

3. Move from discussion into prayer. There's a prayer included in the material which you could use at the end.

4. Encourage the group to use the daily readings in the days between sessions. The readings expand and build on the topic of Communion covered in the DVD and focus especially on how our current understanding of Communion relates to the Jewish Passover ceremony. If the group members are not used to daily Bible reading, encourage them to develop this habit. If the group members are already into a routine of daily Bible reading and prayer you might want to discuss how best to work these new readings into their time.

5. You could start the next session by reviewing how the group found the daily readings. What did they learn? Do they have questions to raise? How did God speak?

This resource may require meeting for an additional time to discuss the final week's readings and discuss any remaining thoughts and questions which you might have previously run out of time to discuss. You may also want to simply draw the series to a close and spend some time going over what each member has learnt.

Communion as c

ICEBREAKER

• Do you recall the community in which you first took bread and wine in remembrance of Christ? Was it a positive experience?

FOR GROUP DISCUSSION

• We have noted the 'five C's in Communion': community, commemoration, covenant, celebration and commitment. Which of these has been most meaningful to you in your Christian life so far?

• Do you share 'the peace' together when your community celebrates Communion? Do you know why? Explore the scriptural origins of this act together.

mmunity

- The early church not only shared meals, but also shared their lives together. What might the barriers for this be today?

- What do we miss when we don't draw close to brothers and sisters with whom we share Communion?

- Can you think of an occasion when resolving a difference led to closer fellowship with someone?

• In addition to celebrating Communion, what other activities have helped you draw closer to other Christians?

Dear Lord, we are sad for the ways in which Your Church has been divided and for the attitudes and beliefs that have contributed to the division. Forgive us our sins and give us grace to love all those with whom we celebrate Communion. Amen.

An urgent need

For reading & meditation – 1 Corinthians 10:14–22

*'you cannot have a part in both the Lord's
table and the table of demons.' (v21)*

I hope that *Eat Pray Share* will draw us in thought and spirit towards
the great sacrifice that Jesus made for us on the cross of Calvary. We
will be considering the Communion table, a central feature of most
Christian churches, at which is celebrated the event variously described
as 'The Sacrament', 'Holy Communion', 'The Lord's Supper', 'The
Lord's Table', 'The Eucharist' or 'The Breaking of Bread'.

Almost every Christian participates from time to time in a service
of Communion, but how many of us, I wonder, understand the rich
significance that lies behind the simple act of taking and sharing the
bread and drinking the wine? Over the years I have inquired of many
people of all denominations as to how they understand the act of
'Holy Communion' and, generally speaking, I have discovered only a
superficial understanding. Why is it that an event which was intended
by Jesus to be a source of continuous spiritual enrichment is, for many,
nothing more than a ritual? *I am convinced that one of the most urgent
needs of the contemporary Christian Church is to return meaning to the
Communion.*

When we fail to appreciate the meaning of this deeply significant
act, then our meeting together around the 'Lord's Table' will have little
impact on our lives – individually or collectively. I believe that those
who see it as nothing more than a sentimental forget-me-not service
will, as a result, be spiritually poorer. Those who see it for what it is – a
service of deep spiritual significance – will be continually enriched,
enlightened and satisfied.

**My Father and my God, help me to see, as I begin these meditations,
that whatever table I sit at, none is more sacred and special
than Your table. Reveal to me more clearly than ever before its
meaning and its purpose. In Christ's name I pray. Amen.**

The law of first occurrence

For reading & meditation – Matthew 26:17–30

*'While they were eating, Jesus took bread, gave thanks
and broke it, and gave it to his disciples' (v26)*

Today we ask ourselves: if the Christian Church is greatly in need of
returning meaning to the Communion, where do we start? There is
a law of biblical interpretation known as 'the law of first occurrence'
which states that whenever you wish to understand a truth of
Scripture, you should examine in detail the first occasion when that
truth is mentioned.

If we are to understand the deep meaning that lies in the
commemorative act of Holy Communion, then our first task must
be to focus our attention on the very first Communion service in
history – the one conducted by Jesus that famous night in the
Upper Room. When a jeweller wants to show off a diamond to its
best advantage, he often puts it on a background of black velvet.
There, as natural or artificial light strikes it, the diamond catches
fire, whereupon its beauty and brilliance is greatly magnified and its
value made more apparent.

The Lord's Supper is like that diamond. It needs to be prised from its
traditional setting, where, by reason of endless controversy, it borders
on becoming lacklustre, and set against the velvet of the blackest night
in history – the night before Jesus was crucified. It is only there, in its
original setting, with the light of the Holy Spirit falling upon it, that
it yields its true and proper meaning. And I say again – if we do not
understand what happened at that very first Communion service, then
we will not be able to understand what it means for us now – here in
the twenty-first century.

**Dear God, thank You that it is Your Holy Spirit who illuminates
the truth. As a diamond catches fire, help me to understand
the brilliance of the act of Holy Communion. Amen.**

The Christ of the unexpected

For reading & meditation – John 2:13–25; 6:1–14

*'at the Passover Feast, many people saw the miraculous signs
he was doing and believed in his name.' (John 2:23)*

Before we begin a detailed examination of the first Communion
service in history, we refer briefly to the event that led to the institution
of what we now call 'Holy Communion' – namely, the feast of the
Passover. More will be said about this later, but the feast of the Passover
was the annual celebration of the night when God passed over the land
of Egypt and spared the firstborn of the children of Israel. It is still
celebrated by many Jews today.

It is probable that Jesus and His disciples had shared together in
the ceremony of the Passover on previous occasions, but we cannot
be certain. According to John, we know, however, that the disciples
had been with Him on two previous Passover festivals, and on both
these occasions, something unexpected and unusual had taken
place. On the first occasion, Jesus entered the Temple and in an act of
righteous indignation, proceeded to empty it of the moneychangers
who, He said, had turned His Father's house into 'a den of robbers'
(Luke 19:46). On the second occasion, He performed the miracle of the
feeding of the 5,000 (John 6:1–14).

I wonder, as once again the Passover approached, did the disciples
think to themselves: what surprises will the Master have for us on this
occasion? Will He once again do the unexpected and the unusual? It is
only conjecture, of course, but if this thought did arise in their minds,
they could have had no idea that they were about to be witnesses of
the most central Passover of all time, and be observers of an event that
would change the entire course of history.

**Heavenly Father, help me never to forget that You are
the God of the unusual and the unexpected. Show me
that when I follow You and Your Son, there are surprises
around every corner. Thank You, dear Father. Amen.**

Believing the Master's word

For reading & meditation – Luke 22:7–13
'They left and found things just as Jesus had told them.' (v13)

If, as we said yesterday, the disciples were wondering whether Jesus might once again perform the unusual and unexpected at the Passover feast, we can see from our passage today that they were not left wondering for long. At the beginning of the Passover, the Master issues them with a set of very unusual and unexpected instructions. 'Go into the city', He tells them, 'and you will see a man carrying a pitcher of water; follow him and he will take you to a room where we will celebrate the Passover together' (paraphrased from Luke 22:10–12).

There can be little doubt that the knowledge Jesus had concerning the man and the room was supernatural, but there is another point to be noted here: that is, the complete and utter confidence the disciples had in the word and command of Jesus. No one remonstrated with Him and said, 'But, Master, men don't usually carry pitchers of water – that is normally a task that women perform.' Neither did they say, 'Lord, what will this man think of us when we attempt to follow him?' The disciples had obviously learned to trust the word of Jesus and to act without questioning His commands.

That is a lesson every one of us sorely needs to learn. How often things go wrong in our lives because we quibble over Jesus' words. I wonder, am I talking to someone at this very moment who is hesitating or drawing back from something the Master has shown you that He wants you to do? If so, then let me give you the word that Mary, Jesus' mother, once gave to a group of interested but hesitant people: 'Do whatever he tells you' (John 2:5).

Loving Father, how expertly You put Your finger on my need. I am often afraid to do what You ask me to do – afraid that it might not be in my best interests or that I might make a fool of myself. Help me see how foolish that is. Amen.

The 'Pass-over'

For reading & meditation – Exodus 12:1–13

*'The blood will be a sign for you ... and when I see
the blood, I will pass over you.' (v13)*

If we are to comprehend the real meaning of the Communion, then we
must begin to understand what the feast of the Passover was all about,
for it was out of that that the first Communion service emerged.
During the time of Israel's bondage and slavery in Egypt, God spoke to
Pharaoh through Moses and warned him that on a certain day, at the
hour of midnight, He was going to pass through the land and strike
down every firstborn. There was to be no discrimination between
human beings and animals, or between different social classes – every
firstborn would die.

God then devised a plan whereby the firstborn of His own people,
the Israelites, would be protected. Each Israelite was to choose a lamb
(a year-old male without defect) and kill it. They were then to take
some of the lamb's blood, dip a branch of hyssop in it and sprinkle
it on the lintel and side posts of their front door. They were not to
go out of the house at all that night. Having shed and sprinkled the
blood, they must shelter under it. At midnight God passed through the
land, and in every house that did not have a blood-sprinkled door, the
firstborn died. The God who passed *through* Egypt in judgment passed
over every blood-marked dwelling place – hence the term, 'Pass-over'.

It is worth noting – if rubies or some other precious stones had
gleamed like red flames from every door, it would not have saved the
firstborn of the children of Israel. God had decreed that it was only by
the shedding of blood that they were to be saved. If the Israelites had
stumbled here, they would never have made it to this point in history.

**My Father, I realise that this question of redemption by blood
is of vital importance, even for us today. Help me to grasp the
immensity of the sacrifice Jesus made in shedding His blood
that I might be redeemed. For His name's sake. Amen.**

Communion as c

Icebreaker

- Have you ever forgotten a significant event? If so, what was the consequence?

For group discussion

- Has Jesus ever asked you to do something specific?

- Think of the kinds of commemorative acts you have in your family, church or community. What value do they have?

mmemoration

- Discuss ways in which you can make space in a busy day to remember all that God is, and has done for you.

- What comes into your mind when you think of the presence of Jesus? How is this known to you?

- Do you think that memorials had more meaning to believers who had little written material to help them?

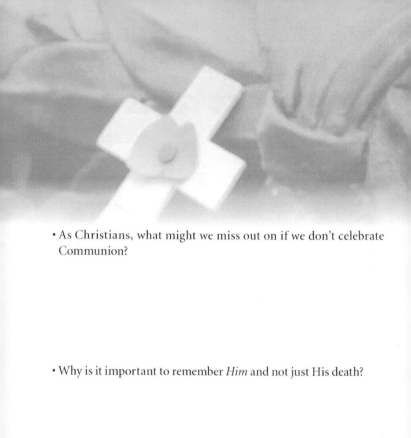

• As Christians, what might we miss out on if we don't celebrate Communion?

• Why is it important to remember *Him* and not just His death?

Dear Lord Jesus, help us to recognise all that You are as we celebrate Communion. We thank You for the gift of Your life and the pain that You suffered for us. We thank You too for Your present resurrected life at the Father's right hand and the victory that we enjoy as Your followers. May we rejoice in this renewed life as we live daily in Your grace. Amen.

The meaning of Passover

For reading & meditation – Exodus 12:14–28

'This is a day you are to commemorate; for the generations to come ... celebrate it as a festival to the LORD' (v14)

As an understanding of the feast of the Passover is a vital key to comprehending the meaning that lies behind the act of 'Holy Communion', we must spend another day exploring it further. On Passover night itself, the Israelites were bidden to feast on a roasted lamb, with bitter herbs and unleavened bread, and they were to do so with their cloak tucked into their belt, their sandals on their feet and their staff in their hand, ready to make a quick departure from the land of slavery.

The night of the Passover was so important that it marked the beginning of a new year for Israel – 'This month is to be ... the first month of your year' (12:2). From that day to this, the Jewish religious new year begins with *Pesach* – the Hebrew word for 'Passover'. God gave the Israelites an instruction that this feast should be commemorated throughout the generations to come, and families should explain to their children what the whole ceremony meant: 'It is the Passover sacrifice to the LORD, who passed over the houses of the Israelites in Egypt and spared our homes when he struck the Egyptians' (v27).

This celebration was to last seven days and was known as the Feast of Unleavened Bread, during which time the Israelites were to remind themselves that their deliverance from Egypt's bondage had been planned by Jehovah, purchased by blood and implemented by divine power. Being a redeemed people, this meant that they belonged to the Almighty in a special way and were therefore to be consecrated to His service and be an illustration to the world of what redeemed people should be like.

Father, the implications of all this go deep into my soul as I reflect on whether I am an illustration to the world of what a redeemed person should be like. I take a step closer to You today. Make me what I ought to be. In Jesus' name. Amen.

The Passover table

For reading & meditation – Mark 14:12–16
'So they prepared the Passover.' (v16)

Having seen what the feast of the Passover means and why it was to be celebrated annually, we return now to the details of the last Passover feast which Jesus commemorated with His disciples. Upon finding the room in which the Master purposed to celebrate the Passover, the disciples began at once to make the preparations for the feast.

Although every one of the four Gospels contains an account of the Last Supper, we are not given any details as to how the feast was prepared and what items were placed on the Passover table. We know from the instructions given by God in the Old Testament and tradition that certain items would be laid out on the table. There would have been a supply of bitter herbs – a reminder of the suffering that their forefathers went through in Egypt. Another item would have been a bowl of salt water to remind them of the tears that were shed during the years of bondage and slavery. A further item would have been grated apple mixed with nuts and made into a paste (called *charoseth*), which would resemble the colour of clay and thus remind them of the endless amount of bricks that were made in Egypt.

Yet another item would have been unleavened bread, the absence of yeast symbolising the haste of that unforgettable night and also the need to break with the leaven of evil. On the table, too, would have been an egg symbolising new life, candles to remind them of the worship that went on in the tabernacle, wine to symbolise the shedding of blood, and last but not least – a roasted lamb. All this had a supreme and important purpose – the event must be kept alive in the memory of Israel. For great events ought to never be forgotten.

Lord Jesus, help me see the value of keeping alive in my memory the great Passover act that You accomplished for me on Calvary. May the wonder of it reverberate within my being yet again this day. In Your dear name I ask it. Amen.

Great enough to be humble

For reading & meditation – John 13:1–17

'he poured water into a basin and began to wash his disciples' feet' (v5)

We move on now to focus our attention on the interesting and dramatic events that went on in the Upper Room in Jerusalem where Jesus observed the Passover feast with His disciples. Picture the scene with me. It is dusk, and Jesus and His disciples are reclining around a low table in an atmosphere that is heavy with unborn events. Outside a storm is brewing that will eventually engulf the Son of God and sweep Him towards the cross. Jesus had already seen the sun set for the last time. In less than 18 hours, His limbs would be stretched on what one writer calls those 'grisly timbers of torture'; within 24 hours, He would be dead.

Evidently no servant was in attendance to wash the feet of those present – a usual courtesy of the day – so Jesus rises from the table, strips off His outer clothing and, taking a towel and a bowl of water, proceeds to wash the disciples' feet. We said earlier that the disciples would face many surprises at this last crucial Passover. This was another – in the form of the Saviour who stooped to wash their feet.

Isn't it interesting that *none* of the disciples volunteered for that lowly task? They were so unsure of themselves that they dared not be humble – such an action might have caused them to lose their frail sense of identity. Jesus, on the other hand, had such a clear sense of identity – knowing that He had come from God and was going to God – that He could choose to be humble. How sad that the disciples were willing to fight over a throne, but not over a towel. Things don't seem to have changed much in 20 centuries, do they?

Gracious and loving Father, forgive me that I too am more interested in a throne than a towel; more concerned about status than I am about serving. Father, help me become more like Jesus. For His own dear name's sake. Amen.

Humility – a choice

For reading & meditation – Matthew 20:17–28

'the Son of Man did not come to be served, but to serve,
and to give his life as a ransom for many.' (v28)

We said yesterday that Jesus was so conscious of greatness that He could afford to be humble. What does this really mean? Consider once again the account given by the apostle John: 'Jesus knew that the Father had put all things under his power, and that he had come from God and was returning to God; so he got up from the meal, took off his outer clothing, and wrapped a towel round his waist … he poured water into a basin and began to wash his disciples' feet' (John 13:3–5).

Notice how John, under the inspiration of the Holy Spirit, sees right into the mind of Jesus before He stoops down to wash the disciples' feet. And what does he see? He sees Jesus' consciousness of His own greatness – 'Jesus knew … that he had come from God and was returning to God'. The consciousness of greatness is the secret of humility. Those who do not have a high sense of their worth and value in God can never, in the true sense of the word, be humble. Their 'humility' borders more on self-belittlement. They do not *choose* to be humble, for more often than not, they are forced into situations which they can do very little about except say to themselves, 'Well, now that I am here, I will be humble.'

Humility is always a choice – a choice which arises out of a high sense of one's worth and value. Look at this phrase: 'Jesus knew that the Father had put all things under his power.' Everything was under His power! And what did He do with that power? He used it to take a towel, pour water into a bowl and wash the disciples' feet. Knowing who He was made Him great – and humble. Great because humble, and humble because great.

Father, if it is true that the consciousness of greatness is the secret of humility, then give me a vision today, not only of Your greatness, but of my greatness also – my greatness in You. In Christ's name I pray. Amen.

'No, not my feet!'

For reading & meditation – 1 Peter 5:1–11

*'Clothe (apron) yourselves, all of you, with humility
[as the garb of a servant]' (v5, Amplified Bible)*

We spend another day looking at that moving moment when Jesus
began washing the disciples' feet. I can imagine that by the time Jesus
got to Simon Peter, the arguing and small talk that had been going on
among the disciples would have diminished. No doubt they began to
realise how slow and insensitive they had been not to take the servant's
role themselves. But as Jesus bends before Peter, the disciple almost
shouts, 'No! Not my feet! You shall never wash my feet.'

Is that what humility is – refusing to let Jesus wash one's feet? Of
course not. In fact, it sometimes takes more humility to be ministered
to than it does to minister. You see, when we are always giving out to
others, it is fairly easy to cover up our pride, but when we are put on
the receiving end and others are ministering to us, then our pride has
nowhere to hide. Jesus said some strong words to Peter at this point:
'Unless I wash you, you have no part with me.' This firm statement
penetrated Peter's defences, but rather than face his pride, he found
another way out – the way of overreaction: 'Then, Lord ... not just my
feet but my hands and my head as well!'

After Jesus had brought about some balance in Peter's life and
had finished washing the disciples' feet, He sat back at the table and
gave them this instruction, 'Now that I, your Lord and Teacher, have
washed your feet, you also should wash one another's feet.' Notice the
words – 'one another's feet'. Had He said, 'You should wash my feet',
every disciple would have clamoured for the privilege. Who wouldn't
stand in line to wash the Saviour's feet? But 'one another's feet' – ah,
that's different. That puts obedience to its maximum test.

**Lord Jesus Christ, You who stooped to wash the disciples' feet, put in
my heart this very day that same spirit of humility and love. Make of
me what You can, dear Lord. For Your own dear name's sake. Amen.**

Communion as c

Icebreaker

• What promises have you made in your life that really matter?

For group discussion

• If the old covenant was going to be superseded, why not bring in the new covenant first?

• What do we learn from the old covenant that makes it valuable in our appreciation of the new?

venant

• Why do you think Jeremiah's prophecy of the new covenant did not mention blood at all?

• Why did Jesus choose the Passover meal as the basis for the Communion meal?

- Knowing that blood is an off-putting idea, why is there so much 'running through' the Bible? Won't it put people off?

Dear Lord, we are grateful that we live under a new covenant, that Your Son's blood was shed on our behalf once and for all and that we can look back with gratitude to the sacrifice of Jesus, knowing that our sins are remembered no more. Amen.

Judas the betrayer

For reading & meditation – John 13:18–30

'As soon as Judas had taken the bread,
he went out. And it was night.' (v30)

We look now at another scene from the great drama that was enacted in the Upper Room on that first Maundy Thursday – Jesus' confrontation with Judas. It must have come as a great surprise to Judas when the Master made the announcement that there was someone present who was about to betray Him. E.F. Kevan says, 'It was the custom at the Passover feast for the presiding father, if there was an especially honoured guest, to break off a large piece of bread and give it to him first. It was that large piece that Jesus gave to Judas.'

As soon as Judas received the bread from Jesus' hand, we read that 'Satan entered into him'. He then went out to put into action his plan of betrayal and the Scripture cryptically says, 'And it was night.' Night in Jerusalem, and night in his soul! How it must have hurt Jesus to have been betrayed by one of His own disciples. In this hard and cruel world, people expect to be shot at by their enemies, but no one except a cynic, expects to be shot at by his friends.

Did you know it is thought that the origin of the superstition concerning the number thirteen stems from this scene in the Gospels? Thirteen sat down at the Last Supper, and one of them was a traitor. Superstitious people have dreaded the number thirteen ever since. Have you ever been betrayed? It's not easy to remain unembittered when someone who has stood at your side and claimed to be your friend lets you down. Jesus, despite the pain that the knowledge of Judas' betrayal caused Him, did not allow it to deter Him from ministering to the other disciples. Nor, too, must we.

Lord Jesus, I am thankful that You make it possible for me to go on even when I am in pain. And whenever I am let down, help me to drink deeply of Your own determination and keep on ministering to others. For Your name's sake. Amen.

Accountant turned embezzler

For reading & meditation – 1 Timothy 6:3–19
'For the love of money is a root of all kinds of evil.' (v10)

Today we ask ourselves: who was Judas Iscariot and how do we explain his involvement in the betrayal of Jesus? It is believed by most Bible commentators that Judas was a Judean, and if this was true, then he would have been the only member of the apostolic band who was a southerner. Observe that, for it is not unimportant. Eleven of Christ's disciples were Galileans and only one came from the south. This would have meant that not only did Judas speak with a different accent, but also his views and outlook on things would have been quite different from the rest of the group. This might have put him a little bit on his own from the start. I am saying this, I hasten to add, not to excuse him, but to explain him.

It seems also that he was a man with a commercial mind, for he was appointed to be the treasurer of the party – the 'keeper of the money bag' (John 12:6). The little company, as it moved from place to place, needed someone to handle simple purchases, and as Judas possessed some business acumen, he was the one chosen for the task. But Judas was not just a man with a business mind: he was also a man with a covetous heart. We are told that he had been dipping into the money bag for a long time before he took the traitorous step of betraying Jesus.

With some natures, there is nothing so holy that money cannot besmirch it. Watch money – it is so terribly useful and yet so terribly dangerous. What is dangerous is not the money itself, but the way in which it can tempt us to become attached to it. When money becomes our god, then a susceptible personality is the price we pay for the worship of that god.

Gracious and loving heavenly Father, show me how to cut out of my nature that 'root of all evil' – the love of money. I want money to be my servant, not my master. Help me, dear Lord, in this quest. For Jesus' sake I pray. Amen.

A free agent

For reading & meditation – Psalm 41:1–13

'Even my close friend, whom I trusted ...
has lifted up his heel against me.' (v9)

We spend one more day discussing Judas and his involvement in the betrayal of Jesus. Some Christian writers have expressed great sympathy for Judas. They feel he had an unfair deal in his life and has suffered from a bad press ever since. 'After all,' they say, 'if Jesus had to die, somebody had to betray Him. So why blame Judas? He was but the tool of providence, the victim of predestination.'

The Bible certainly indicates that Jesus foreknew that He would be betrayed by him (see John 6:64), but foreknowledge is not the same thing as foreordination. I know the sun will rise tomorrow, but my knowing it does not make it rise. The foreknowledge that Jesus had concerning Judas did not compel him to act the way he did – he was a free agent in it all. Judas got involved in the act of betrayal by following the same method that every one of us follows when we commit sin – first we are tempted, then, instead of showing it the door, we bring it into our living room and entertain it. After that, the temptation is more difficult to resist and then it is just a step downward into sin.

However strong the various influences were around Judas, there must have been a time when he opened himself to them. Jesus clearly regarded him as a responsible agent, for even at the last minute in the Upper Room, He carefully worded His statement so that Judas had an opportunity to recant. So underhand was this action of Judas that throughout history, whenever Maundy Thursday comes around, the first thing that comes into our mind is this – it was the night on which our Saviour was betrayed.

Father, I ask one thing, not that I shall be preserved from being betrayed, but that I shall be preserved from betraying others. And above all – from betraying You. Make me a person who is not only trusting, but trustworthy. In Jesus' name. Amen.

The order of service

For reading & meditation – Exodus 13:1–10

'You must keep this ordinance at the appointed time year after year.' (v10)

We turn now from looking at some of the personalities who were present in the Upper Room when Jesus conducted the first Communion service to focus on the Master Himself. I wonder how Jesus felt as He realised that He was setting up His own memorial service? What were the things He emphasised as He celebrated this Passover of all Passovers? Where was the transition point when the Passover feast took on the nature of a new commemorative act? These are some of the questions we will come to grips with over the days that lead up to Good Friday – but first let's reflect together on the way in which the Passover meal was conducted.

None of the four Gospel writers give exact and detailed accounts of the traditions that they followed during a Passover meal – they focused more on the highlights of that memorable evening – so we have to depend on sources outside of Scripture for information concerning this. I am drawing therefore on the writings of Jewish authors and the practice of many Jews today, as I describe to you the tradition of a Passover celebration.

Just after dusk on the night of the Passover, a Jewish family gather around a table on which has been laid out the various items I described for you a few days ago. The meal begins with the father holding up the first of the four cups that are on the table and praying over it, then all drink from it. This is called the 'Cup of Kiddush', meaning separation or sanctification. It was the cup that separated this meal from all other meals and marked it out as being different.

Loving Father, as I come to study the order in which the Passover feast is conducted, help me to see the ways in which it reveals Your great plan of eternal salvation. In Jesus' name I pray. Amen.

The meaning of the four cups

For reading & meditation – Exodus 6:1–13
'I have heard the groaning of the Israelites ...
and I have remembered my covenant.' (v5)

We continue looking at the manner in which the Passover meal was conducted during the time of Christ, and is still conducted by Jews today. We said yesterday that the meal commenced with the drinking of the first of four cups – the 'Cup of Kiddush'. The four cups were reminders of the four promises of Exodus 6:6–7: (1) I will bring you out from under the yoke of the Egyptians; (2) I will free you from being slaves to them; (3) I will redeem you with an outstretched arm and with mighty acts of judgment; (4) I will take you as my own people and I will be your God.

After the drinking of the first cup, the host would take a bowl of water and a towel and pass them around the table so that all could wash their hands. He would then draw attention to the bitter herbs and the bowl of salt water that were on the table, which they would all be invited to taste – a reminder of the bitterness of slavery in Egypt and of the tears that had been shed so profusely by their forefathers.

Then the main course would be brought out, which consists of roast lamb, although it would not be eaten yet. The family would be reminded that it was through the shed blood of a lamb that their homes had been protected when the destroyer passed through Egypt. Their attention would be drawn, too, to the presence of the unleavened bread on the table and how they had to leave behind them all reminders of the culture when fleeing from Egypt, including the leaven for their bread. Then would come the second eating of bitter herbs, a further reminder of the bitterness of slavery. A further benediction was then offered in gratitude to God for His deliverance on that dark and fateful night.

My God, I sense that though wondrous and miraculous, that first Passover night was but a dress rehearsal for another and greater Passover – the deliverance wrought through our Lord's sacrifice on the cross. I am eternally grateful. Amen.

Communion as c

Icebreaker

• Think back to your most memorable celebratory meal. What did you have to eat? What made it different from regular meals?

For group discussion

• Why do you think Communion services sometimes appear to be sombre?

• What does it mean to 'feed on Christ'? (See John 6:35.)

ebration

- How does your church community celebrate good news? Does this impact your wider community?

- Does true and sincere thankfulness and celebration have to be exuberant?

• Spend some time talking about how you might 'celebrate' communion more fully – both individualy and collectively?

Dear Lord, when we reflect on the all that You have done for us, we are truly grateful. May Your Spirit encourage our hearts that we may rejoice afresh in our salvation and truly celebrate all that You have done. Amen.

The eating of the lamb

For reading & meditation – Exodus 15:1–19

*'By the power of your arm they will be as still as a
stone – until your people pass by, O Lord' (v16)*

We continue looking at the way in which the Passover meal was
celebrated, as it is an important and necessary background to our
understanding of the Lord's Supper. After the second eating of the
bitter herbs would come the drinking of the second cup, which was
called the 'Cup of Haggadah' or the 'Cup of Explanation'. The father
would once again lead the family in the drinking of this cup.

At this point, the youngest son in the family would be prompted
formally to ask a series of questions starting with, 'Why is this night
different from all other nights?' The head of the household would
then give a potted history of Israel right down to the deliverance of
the Passover, explaining how this demonstrated God's everlasting
power and mercy. Following this he would begin the singing of the
first part (Psalms 113 and 114) of what was called the Egyptian Hallel
– the name given to the group of psalms of praise from Psalm 113 to
Psalm 118, which were used for Passover.

Next came a second act of hand washing. The host would wash his
hands and then prepare a 'sop' – a piece of unleavened bread filled with
lamb and dipped in the paste called the *charoseth*. He would give the
sop to the honoured guest on his left, then to others sitting around the
table. It was this 'sop' Jesus offered to Judas (in place of the honoured
guest) who, at this point in the Last Supper, left to betray Him
(John 13:26–30). Following this would come the eating of the meal, the
roasted lamb, which by tradition had to be wholly eaten. Anything left
over was to be destroyed and not used for a common meal.

**Loving Father, as I follow these procedures, I see how
painstakingly You prepared Your people for that Passover of
all Passovers. Understanding each part will help me gain more
from each Lord's Supper I celebrate. Thank You. Amen.**

'The Hallel'

For reading & meditation – Psalm 136:1–26

'Give thanks to the Lord, for he is good. His love endures for ever.' (v1)

We spend one more day exploring the formalities of the Passover meal. Once the lamb had been eaten, then came the drinking of the third cup – called the 'Cup of Thanksgiving'. This cup was served with a piece of unleavened bread. Once the cup had been drunk, the host would then give thanks for the meal that they had eaten, after which would follow the singing of the rest of the Egyptian Hallel – Psalms 115 to 118. Then the fourth cup would be drunk, whereupon the family would sing what is known as 'The Hallel' – the psalm before us today. The singing of 'The Hallel' would bring the Passover meal to its conclusion.

We cannot be certain, of course, whether or not Jesus followed this precise pattern at the Passover feast He celebrated with His disciples, although I think we can safely assume that apart from those moments when He gave the Passover a new direction, He did. It's interesting to note that none of the Gospels go into detail about the exact location of the room, the position of the disciples around our Lord, or the number of artefacts upon the table – all these things seemed to be considered as relatively unimportant.

What was important – and every Gospel writer recorded it – was the stunning revelation that Jesus gave concerning a new commemorative act that would become the ultimate Passover feast. No wonder Jesus said, at the beginning of the meal, 'I have eagerly desired to eat this Passover with you before I suffer' (Luke 22:15). He longed to let them know that the story of His death had been hidden all the time within the Passover celebration – waiting to be revealed.

Blessed Lord Jesus, I bow in adoration and worship before You as I contemplate the eagerness with which You reached out to the cross. 'All this Thou didst for me – what can I now do for Thee?' Amen.

Born to die

For reading & meditation – John 12:20–36

'No, it was for this very reason I came to this hour.' (v27)

Now that we have familiarised ourselves with the traditional manner in which the feast of the Passover was conducted, we ask ourselves: what must have been going on in the heart and mind of the Master as He shared the Passover meal with His disciples? He was clearly aware of the fact that His death was imminent, for, as we saw yesterday, He had said, 'I have eagerly desired to eat this Passover with you before I suffer.'

The astonishing thing is that even though our Lord knew that within 24 hours He would be dead and buried, it was clear that He was thinking of His mission, not as something that was past, but as something that yet awaited Him. Normally, a person who has lived barely half the allotted span of life, when told that he is about to die, is plunged into deep depression. Kübler-Ross, the famous anthropologist who made a special study of the reactions people go through when they know they are about to die, said that there are five clear stages through which a person passes when confronted by the news that death is imminent.

I watched my wife go through these five stages when her doctors informed her that her sickness was terminal. But I find nothing of this in the heart and mind of Jesus. He suffered intense grief in the Garden of Gethsemane but, as we shall see, this was not because He was unprepared or unwilling to die. The cross was not something our Lord ever tried to avoid: it was the reason why He came. He saw the cross not as the end of His mission, but as the accomplishment of it – His lifelong goal.

Blessed Lamb of God, slain from the foundation of the world, give me an ever-increasing consciousness of the love that led You to leave the eternal throne and die on the cross for me. I am so deeply, deeply thankful. Amen.

Startling vehemence

For reading & meditation – Matthew 16:21–28

'Jesus began to explain to his disciples that he must go to Jerusalem and suffer many things' (v21)

We said yesterday that Christ's death was not something He wanted to avoid: indeed it was the very reason why He came into the world. He was born to die.

Do you know that great painting by Holman Hunt entitled 'The Shadow of Death'? It depicts the inside of the carpenter's shop in Nazareth and shows Jesus, stripped to the waist, standing by a wooden trestle on which He has put down His awl. He is obviously a little tired and stretches both His arms towards heaven. As He does so, the evening sunlight, flooding in through the open door of the little carpenter's shop, casts a dark shadow in the form of a cross on the wall behind Him. In the foreground can be seen His mother, Mary, who, kneeling among the chips of wood, looks up and is obviously startled as she sees her Son's cross-like shadow on the wall.

Some regard this painting as sickly and sentimental, but the idea it contains is a scriptural one – the cross loomed large in the mind and perspective of Jesus, probably from His earliest days and certainly from the commencement of His ministry. The verse before us today is the first prediction of His passion. There had been passing allusions to it before, but here it is quite clear that Jesus knew He was destined for a cross. And so horrified was He by Peter's insistence that He put the thought away from Him that He addressed him with strange and uncharacteristic words, 'Out of my way, Satan!' (v23, J.B. Phillips). The vehemence was not aimed at Peter, but at the satanic ploy that was sounding through him. Nothing could deter Jesus from going to the cross – for He knew that this was the very reason why He had come.

My Lord and Saviour, I am grateful beyond words that You allowed nothing to deter You from going to Calvary. Help me show the same determination in the face of a lesser cross that may confront me. For Your own dear name's sake. Amen.

The moment of revelation

For reading & meditation – Matthew 26:26-30

*'This is my blood of the covenant, which is poured
out for many for the forgiveness of sins.' (v28)*

We come now to the question which has intrigued Christians in
every century of the Christian Church: at what point in the evening
did Jesus make clear to His disciples that He was instituting His
own commemorative meal? We cannot be absolutely sure, but most
commentators believe it was probably after the drinking of the third
cup – 'The Cup of Thanksgiving'.

There are two reasons for this belief – one is that Paul, in his letter
to the Corinthians, refers to the Communion cup as 'the cup of
thanksgiving' (1 Cor. 10:16). The second is the fact that 'The Cup of
Blessing' was served with a piece of unleavened bread, at which time the
head of the household would say, 'This is the bread of affliction which
our fathers had to eat as they came out of Egypt.' If this was the moment
of revelation, then you can imagine how astonished the disciples must
have been when Jesus said those tremendous and powerful words, 'This
is my body given for you; do this in remembrance of me', and 'This
cup is the new covenant in my blood, which is poured out for you'
(Luke 22:19-20).

This is the impact of what He was saying – 'Never again need you keep
as the central focus of your worship the memory of your forefathers'
deliverance from Egypt, for I am about to go to my death as the true
Passover sacrifice. From now on, I want you to remember regularly
an even greater event – the giving of my own body and blood for your
redemption.' In a few simple but powerful words, our Lord transformed
an ancient ritual into the world's most wondrous revelation.

**Lord Jesus, as You interpreted the real meaning of the
Passover to those around You that day, help me to interpret the
meaning of Your cross to those around me today. Amen.**

Communion as

Icebreaker

• Make a list of your present commitments. Which is your favourite? Are there any you struggle with?

For group discussion

• Why is it sometimes hard to commit? What is needed in order to encourage your commitment?

• Do you think that having a meal with someone in our culture today ever has the kind of significance it had in Bible times? What would be closest?

nmitment

• Is your commitment to Jesus typically mentioned in the Communion service you attend?

• How often would you like to celebrate Communion?

• What have you discovered having watched this DVD series? Might you now celebrate Communion any differently?

Father God, we thank You for all that Communion means. Thank You for Your Word, which assures us of the reality of Your grace made known in Jesus. May these studies have an impact in our minds and hearts as we share Communion in the future, as individuals and as a Church. For the sake of Christ and His kingdom. Amen.

God's Paschal Lamb

For reading & meditation – Isaiah 53:1–12
'he was led like a lamb to the slaughter' (v7)

We continue drinking in the wonder of that moment when Jesus revealed to His disciples that He was God's Paschal Lamb, His ultimate sacrificial lamb. In a play, a character standing in the wings with the lighting behind him will cast a long shadow across the stage and, by reason of this, will attract the audience's attention. But when the character himself steps on to the stage, whatever degree of interest the shadow aroused is surpassed by the wonder of seeing the character appear personally.

For centuries, Jesus stood in the wings of history, casting His shadow before Him. He can be seen on almost every page of the Old Testament – in the deliverance of Israel from Egypt, in the sacrifices, in the details of the tabernacle, in the ministry of the priesthood, and so on. Throughout the prophetic books, predictions concerning the coming Messiah give the shadow more detail. Finally, 400 years after Old Testament times, John the Baptist made the declaration, 'Look, the Lamb of God, who takes away the sin of the world!' (John 1:29). At last, the shadow had substance.

Notice the words, 'the Lamb of God, who takes away the *sin of the world*' (my emphasis). The Old Testament shows a progressive revelation as related to the offering of a lamb: first a lamb atoned for an individual, as in the case of Isaac; then for a family, as at the first Passover; then for a nation, as on the Day of Atonement. The world waited for the day when a lamb would come whose sacrifice would take away not just the sins of an individual, a family or even a nation, but the sins of the entire world. Now that day had arrived. And the sacrifice? None other than Jesus – God's Paschal Lamb.

Gracious Father, I am so thankful that before ever there was a man, there was a lamb. For Jesus, Your Son, is the Lamb who was slain from the foundation of the world. I am eternally grateful. Amen.

Where God puts the emphasis

For reading & meditation – Hebrews 9:11–28
*'he entered the Most Holy Place once for all by his own
blood, having obtained eternal redemption.' (v12)*

We must meditate a little further on that wondrous moment when Jesus
revealed Himself to His disciples as the Paschal Lamb and gave them
clear and definite instructions for His own memorial service. Reflect
with me on the deep importance of what He was saying. His memorial
was not to be a single occasion, like our modern-day memorial services
– the final tribute of loved ones and friends – but it was to be a regular
meal, or service, or both. He told them also that He desired this act of
memorial to be repeated: 'Do this in remembrance of me.'

What were they to do? They were to follow His actions and use the
words He Himself had used when He had broken the bread. I always
feel myself that something is missing in a Communion service when
there is any departure from the act of taking, breaking, blessing,
identifying and sharing the bread and the wine. But what do the bread
and wine signify? The words Jesus spoke on that night make it crystal
clear; of the bread, He said, 'This is my body given for you', and of the
wine, 'This cup is the new covenant in my blood, which is poured out
for you.'

John Stott said of this moment, 'The bread did not stand for His
living body as He reclined with them at the table, but His body as it
was shortly to be "given" for them in death. Similarly, the wine did not
stand for His blood as it flowed in His veins while He spoke to them,
but His blood which was shortly to be poured out for them in death.'
It is clear that it is not so much by His life, but by His death, that Jesus
wishes to be remembered. His life is important, but much more His
death. It has accomplished so much for us.

**Mighty God, help me to put the emphasis where You have put
it, not so much on my Saviour's life, spotless and exemplary
though it was, but on His sacrificial and atoning death. I ask
this in and through His peerless and precious name. Amen.**

The centrality of the cross

For reading & meditation – Galatians 6:1–15

'May I never boast except in the cross of our Lord Jesus Christ' (v14)

We continue meditating on the fact that although the life of our Lord was supremely important, the place where God puts the highest emphasis is on His sacrificial and atoning death. Modern-day theologians who bypass the death of Christ and focus instead on such things as His exemplary life, His powerful words, His great miracles and so on, have their priorities all wrong. The emphasis which Jesus placed on His own death shows quite clearly that He regarded this as central to His purpose in coming to the world. Not that His exemplary life and character have no purpose – they most certainly do – but had He not died on the cross, then we would never have known what it means to be 'saved'.

One commentator puts it like this: 'The Lord's Supper, which was instituted by Jesus, and which is the only regular commemorative act authorised by Him, dramatises neither His birth nor His life, neither His words nor His works, but only His death.' It was by His death that He wished above all else to be remembered. You see, then, how essential the cross is to Christianity. In a day and an age when religionists are attempting to turn the spotlight away from the cross and focus instead on the life and words of Jesus, we must do everything in our power to proclaim the centrality of the cross. No cross – no Christianity; it is as simple as that. I take my stand – and I pray that you do too – with the hymnist who said:

> *Forbid it, Lord, that I should boast*
> *Save in the death of Christ my Lord*
> *All the vain things that charm me most*
> *I sacrifice them to his blood.*
> Isaac Watts (1674–1748)

God my Father, I am so glad that even though I cannot fathom all the mystery of the cross, I can take hold of its saving power. It is sometimes darkness to my intellect, but sunshine to my heart. Thank You, Father. Amen.

Getting the 'me' into Calvary

For reading & meditation – Galatians 2:15–21

'the Son of God, who loved me and gave himself for me.' (v20)

Before we leave the Upper Room and go down with Jesus into Gethsemane, we draw one more concluding lesson from what went on in that memorable first Communion service. It concerns the need for each one of us personally to apply and appropriate the death of Christ for ourselves. If, as we have been saying, it was in the Upper Room that Jesus gave to His disciples an advance dramatisation of His death on the cross, it is important that we see further what this was designed to convey.

The celebration of that first Communion did not just involve Jesus, but it involved all the disciples also. Christ initiated it, but the others took part in it as well. They could hardly have failed to get the message that it was not enough for the bread to be broken and the cup of wine to be handed to them – they had to eat and drink and thus appropriate it for themselves. They were not spectators – they were participants.

What does all this say to us? It says that the death of Christ is the means by which we are saved, but we will not be saved until we receive and appropriate for ourselves the sacrifice He made for us on the cross. This is extremely important, for there are many this Easter who, when they are reminded of Christ's death on the cross, will think that because of that, they are automatically forgiven. That is not so. Unless we do as John Wesley said, and get the 'me' into the cross – Christ died for me – and personally receive His forgiveness by an appropriating act of faith, then the tragic situation is this – it will be as if He never died for us.

Heavenly Father, thank You for reminding me that it is only as I appropriate what Christ did for me on Calvary that I am saved. I have seen it – may millions more come to know it this Easter time. In Jesus' name I pray. Amen.

'Until He comes'

For reading & meditation – Revelation 22:7-21

'Behold, I am coming soon!' (v7)

We remind ourselves, on this our last day together, of what can be described as 'the five c's of Communion' – community, commemoration, covenant, celebration and commitment. Most Christians, irrespective of denomination, will agree that whenever we approach the Lord's table, we must recognise that it is a collective act in which we focus our attention on Christ's redemptive death on Calvary, remind ourselves of its covenant nature, rejoice in the great benefits of the atonement and pledge our loyalty to Him who loved us and gave Himself for us.

There is just one more word I have to say before we close – the Lord's Supper is a wonderful but only a temporary provision for the Christian Church. We shall not celebrate it in eternity, for there faith will be lost in sight – we do it only 'until He comes'. As we move away from the holy table, we carry with us the thrilling thought that just as Jesus came at His first advent, so will He come again at His second advent.

The Lord's Supper commands, therefore, a confident belief in Jesus' second coming; it is the token of our Master's return. Indeed, without that belief it cannot be said to be truly celebrated. So permit me to repeat it once again – the Lord's Supper is 'until He comes'. This compelling verse puts it still more powerfully:

> *And thus that dark betrayal night*
> *With the last advent we unite*
> *By one blest chain of loving rite*
> *Until He come.*

George Rawson (1807–1889)

Father, what can I say? My heart cries out in eager anticipation, 'Come, Lord Jesus.' Amen.

SmallGroup central

All of our small group ideas and resources in one place

Online:
www.smallgroupcentral.org.uk
is filled with free video teaching, tools, articles and a whole host of ideas.

On the road:
A range of seminars themed for small groups can be brought to your local community. Contact us at **hello@smallgroupcentral.org.uk**

In print:
Books, study guides and DVDs covering an extensive list of themes, Bible books and life issues.

Log on and find out more at:
www.smallgroupcentral.org.uk